Take-Along Guide

Birds, Nests and Eggs

by Mel Boring

illustrations by Linda Garrow

NORTHWORD
Minnetonka, Minnesota

DEDICATION

For Katy, my daughter and research assistant, with love

ACKNOWLEDGMENTS

I am grateful to Rita Hirv, Librarian of the Rockford, Iowa Public Library, and Marilyn Buttjer, Children's Librarian at the Charles City, Iowa Public Library. They have helped a lot to make this book, probably without even realizing it.

Books Are Fun

282 Century Pl, Ste 2000
Louisville, CO 80027
booksarefun.com

Illustrations by Linda Garrow / Book design by Lisa Moore

Library of Congress Cataloging-in-Publication Data

Boring, Mel.
  Birds, nests, and eggs / by Mel Boring ; illustrations by Linda Garrow.
      p.   cm. — (Take-along guide)
  Summary: Describes a select list of birds, their nests, and their eggs.
    ISBN 978-1-941822-54-8 (SC)
    1. Birds—Juvenile literature.   2. Birds—Nests—Identification—
  Juvenile literature.   [1. Birds.   2. Birds—Nests.   3. Birds—Eggs.]
  I. Garrow, Linda, ill.   II. Title.   III. Series.
  QL676.2.B67   1996
  598—dc20   95-31570

Printed in China

Printed by Hung Hing Off-Set Printing Co., LTD., China, Nov. 2014 118345

CONTENTS

Birds, Nests and Eggs

INTRODUCTION

W hat makes birds different from other animals is their WINGS. With those powerful wings, they escape enemies, find new supplies of food, and migrate to warmer places so they can survive winter.

Hundreds of years ago, people knew very little about birds. Some even thought birds went to the moon when they migrated. Now we know more about birds, but there is still much to learn, and a lot to enjoy.

The best time to watch birds is when they are most active: between 6 o'clock and 10 o'clock in the morning. In fact, for people who really like to watch birds, there is a bird-counting program called "Project Feeder-Watch." For more information, you can write to:

Coordinator
Project FeederWatch—Cornell University
159 Sapsucker Woods Road
Ithaca, New York 14850

Most birds don't use their nests more than one season. However, birds like robins do return to the same neighborhood every year. One good way to find most bird nests is to watch for birds carrying nest-building materials in their beaks. You will see this most often in spring or early summer. Then follow the bird quietly to its nest.

It's okay to take a close look at a bird's nest. Most birds are not easily disturbed. But DON'T TOUCH the nest or eggs or babies. And, of course, if the birds put up a fuss, leave the nest right away.

This Take-Along Guide and its activities will help you know some of the wonderful birds you can find. You can use the ruler on the back of this book to figure out how big the birds would be up close. You can bring a pencil and use the Scrapbook to draw what you see.

Discover and have fun in the world of Birds, Nests and Eggs!

AMERICAN ROBIN

Bird

The robin's happy "Cheer-up!" seems to sing away winter and bring on spring. You will see the robin on the lawn tugging up earthworms.

Robins also eat caterpillars, beetles, crickets and spiders—and fruits like apples, cherries and raspberries.

With its red-orange chest, the American robin is the bird we know best. The robin is 9 to 11 inches long. Male robins have dark heads. Female robins have dull gray heads and tails, and grayish legs. Young robins have spots on their undersides.

When temperatures reach above 37°F watch for your first robin. This usually happens beginning in March to early April.

Robins migrate south to warmer weather in the fall. In the winter, they gather in huge groups along the Gulf of Mexico.

Nest

Female robins build the nests, but the male sometimes brings her building materials. She weaves a circle of grasses, twigs, scraps of rags and string. Inside the nest, she molds a cup of mud to fit her body. Look for their first nest in April, and the second as late as August.

A robin's first nest will probably be in a pine, cedar, or spruce tree. Look for their second nest in broadleaf trees, like an elm, maple, oak, willow, poplar or apple. They build their nests between 5 and 70 feet from the ground.

You can help a robin build its nest. Dig up some clay-like wet mud and put it in a pan near the trees in your yard.

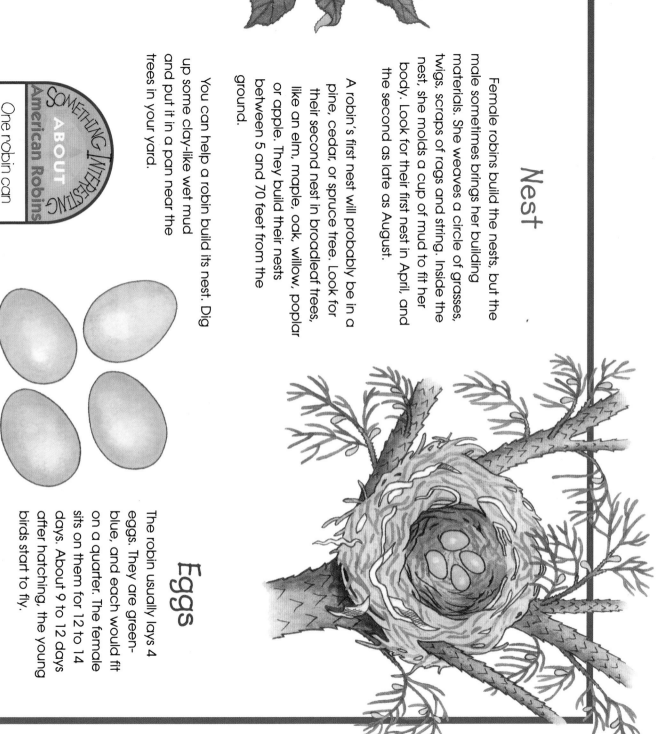

Eggs

The robin usually lays 4 eggs. They are green-blue, and each would fit on a quarter. The female sits on them for 12 to 14 days. About 9 to 12 days after hatching, the young birds start to fly.

HOUSE SPARROW

Bird

Just 150 years ago there were no house sparrows in the United States. Then in 1850, 16 of them were brought to New York City from England. Today there are over 150 million house sparrows in North America. It is one of the most common birds in the world.

House sparrows are very messy birds. And sometimes they chase away other birds like woodpeckers and swallows.

With its chestnut-colored hat and black bib around its neck, the male house sparrow looks dressed up for dinner. Females don't look so dressed up. They are colored streaky brown and dingy white. House sparrows are 5 to 6 inches long.

Though it is a songbird, the house sparrow doesn't have much of a song. It makes a shrill, noisy "cheep" and "chissick."

SOMETHING INTERESTING ABOUT House Sparrows

It will fill its white cheeks with almost anything: seeds, grains, insects, fruits, flowers and scraps.

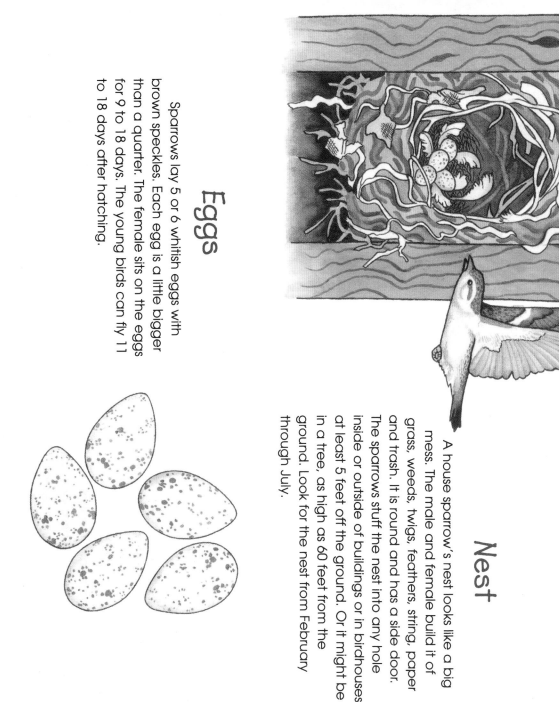

Nest

A house sparrow's nest looks like a big mess. The male and female build it of grass, weeds, twigs, feathers, string, paper and trash. It is round and has a side door. The sparrows stuff the nest into any hole inside or outside of buildings or in birdhouses at least 5 feet off the ground. Or it might be in a tree, as high as 60 feet from the ground. Look for the nest from February through July.

Eggs

Sparrows lay 5 or 6 whitish eggs with brown speckles. Each egg is a little bigger than a quarter. The female sits on the eggs for 9 to 18 days. The young birds can fly 11 to 18 days after hatching.

NORTHERN CARDINAL

Bird

The cardinal is the state bird of more states than any other, and is probably our most popular bird. Male cardinals are easy to spot. They are our only all-red birds with red crests on their heads. They have a black mask across their eyes and under their red-orange beaks. Cardinals are about 8 inches long.

The female cardinal is mostly rosy-yellow, with a few touches of red. Up close, her beak looks as if she is wearing orangeish lipstick.

It is easy to get cardinals to come to feeders because they eat over 100 different kinds of food. Their favorite is sunflower seeds. They also like cracked corn, millet and even peanut butter!

Cardinals sing beautiful songs. You may hear a "Hip-hooray!" or "birdy-birdy-birdy!" Cardinals can sing 28 different songs.

SOMETHING INTERESTING ABOUT Northern Cardinals

Each year cardinals can be found farther north. Now the cardinal has even reached Canada.

Nest

Cardinals begin nesting earlier than most birds. Starting in late March or early April, they might raise 4 broods by the end of summer. The nest is a deep cup of twigs, roots, bark and leaves, lined with grass or animal hair. It is usually hidden in thick shrubs, 2 to 10 feet from the ground.

To figure out where the cardinals are nesting, watch for them both flying into a thicket with nest materials. Or listen for the female singing from the nest. Also, follow the male when he flies to the bush with food in his beak for her.

Eggs

A cardinal egg is about as big as a quarter. It is bluish-white, with reddish-brown spots. The female sits on the 3 or 4 eggs for 12 or 13 days. Young cardinals can fly 10 days after hatching.

BLUE JAY

SOMETHING INTERESTING

ABOUT
Blue Jays

The blue jay is a strong flier. It is able to carry four acorns at a time in its throat and beak. It can easily fly five miles with this load.

Bird

Loud calls of "Jay! Jay!" come from a bird feeder. You know it's a blue jay even before you see it. The other birds all fly away at the blue jay's danger signal—and the clever jay gobbles up all of the sunflower seeds!

With a blue crest and back, bright blue-white-black wings and tail, a blue jay looks as if it has on a blue coat and white underwear. Males and females are colored the same. Jays can grow up to 1 foot long.

The big blue jay hangs around thick shrubs and trees—especially oak—all year long.

Blue jays depend on acorns for food, which they bury for winter. They also like bread, corn and peanuts. Sometimes they eat insects, frogs, salamanders and even mice.

Nest

Though blue jays hang around oaks, their favorite place to nest is in a pine tree, starting in April. They hide their nest in the crotch of the tree. The jay's nest is shaggy-looking—made of sticks and lined with grass and their feathers. Their nest could be anywhere from 5 to 50 feet off the ground.

A male blue jay tries to trick people and other animals from finding its nest by landing at the base of a tree and hopping around and around on the trunk, as if going up a "spiral stairway."

Eggs

Blue jay eggs are green with brown spots. Usually there are 4 or 5 eggs, each a little bigger than a quarter. Both the male and female incubate the eggs, which take about 17 days to hatch. In 17 more days, the young jays start to fly.

NORTHERN ORIOLE

Northern orioles eat beetles, spiders and grasshoppers. They even eat fuzzy caterpillars and wasps. But they seldom eat seeds.

Bird

Northern orioles arrive late in April with a burst of sound and color. Males perch on high places and sing out clear little songs. One is "*Hew-LEE!*"

The male oriole is bright orange on its chest, and black on top, with touches of white on the wings and a black head. Females are olive-brown with duller orange. Orioles are about 8 inches long.

You will find northern orioles around tall shade trees like elms and maples. And once they have paired up, the male and female keep in touch by singing almost all the time.

To get a closer look at orioles, you can use an orange to attract them. Pound a nail halfway into a tree and stick an orange half on it—fruit side out. It usually takes only a few hours for them to find it.

Nest

The northern oriole's nest is usually in a tall shade or fruit tree. It looks like a pouch with a top-hole, hung from the end of a drooping branch. The female weaves the nest together using plant stems, then lines it with fine grass and feathers. It hangs between 6 and 60 feet from the ground.

In their hanging nest, northern oriole babies may be rocked to sleep by the wind. The nest is very strong, however, and often stays in place all through the harsh winter.

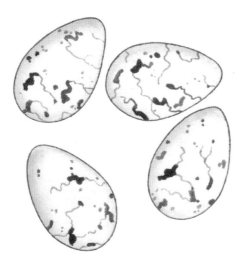

Eggs

One oriole egg is laid each day for 4 to 6 days. The eggs are a bit bigger than nickels. They are gray-white with brown and black blotches. The female sits on the eggs for about 12 to 14 days. Two weeks later the young orioles start to fly.

MAKE A "BLIND" FOR BIRD WATCHING

Birds fly away whenever you go near them. It isn't your scent or bright clothing that frightens them most. It is your movement. Here is how you can get right up next to the birds: Make a tent out of an old sheet or blanket that you can make holes in, or use a big appliance box to hide you from the birds while you are bird watching.

WHAT YOU NEED ▶

- An old sheet or blanket that you have permission to use and cut holes in.

–OR–

- A large appliance box, like the one a stove, refrigerator or air conditioner comes in. But any big box will work, if it will hold two people your size–for you and a friend.

WHAT TO DO ▶

1 Decide where you want to put your "hide." Make sure it will be near where birds usually eat on the grass or at a feeder.

2 Set up a "blind" by draping the sheet or blanket over lawn chairs, picnic table or clothes line. Put rocks on the ends of the material to keep it from blowing around.–OR– Set up the box in an open place on the grass.

3 Cut a watch-hole in the widest side, about 6 inches from the top, in the center. Make the hole 2 inches high and 6 inches wide, big enough for you to look through.

something to do

4 Cut a doorway on the side opposite the watch-hole. Make it big enough for you to crawl through, about 18 inches high and 18 inches wide. Cut it near the center.

5 Don't go near the "blind" for several days. Birds will stay away at first. But when they see that it isn't going to move, they will become used to it, and eat as usual.

6 Then you can creep into your "hide" and wait patiently for the birds to come. Early morning or early afternoon is best. Remember to sit still.

SPECIAL TIPS

▶

Bring binoculars for a closer view of the birds.

Take along a flashlight and this book to read while you wait.

Use the scrapbook pages to write down what you see.

You can even bring along a quiet snack to eat. Raisins and grapes are good treats, but not a crisp, crunchy apple—or crackly potato chips!

THIS END UP

RUBY-THROATED HUMMINGBIRD

Bird

The hummingbird weighs no more than a penny. It is only about 3-1/2 inches long and bathes on a flower leaf with dewdrop water.

Yet, this tiny flying jewel can attack other much bigger birds flying too close to its nest—and win the battle. It can out-fly any bird and fly in any direction, even backward and upside-down at the same time. And hummingbirds are fast fliers. Their average speed is 30 mph, but they have been clocked up to 50 mph.

Ruby-throated hummingbirds have shiny green heads, backs and tails, and gray-white chests. Only the male has the brilliant, glittering, ruby-red throat that gives this humming-bird its name.

Look for hummers beginning in May, when their favorite flowers start to bloom. They sip nectar and snack on small insects around them. They like red flowers best. Especially tube-shape flowers like honeysuckle, morning glory, petunias and lilacs.

Nest

A hummingbird nest is the size of half a golf ball. It is placed near the fork of a tree branch. Look for the nests in apple, maple, oak or pine trees.

Nests are built in May or June, perhaps as high up as 60 feet. The female hummingbird builds it with plant fuzz, lichens and bark. The whole thing is held together with spider web.

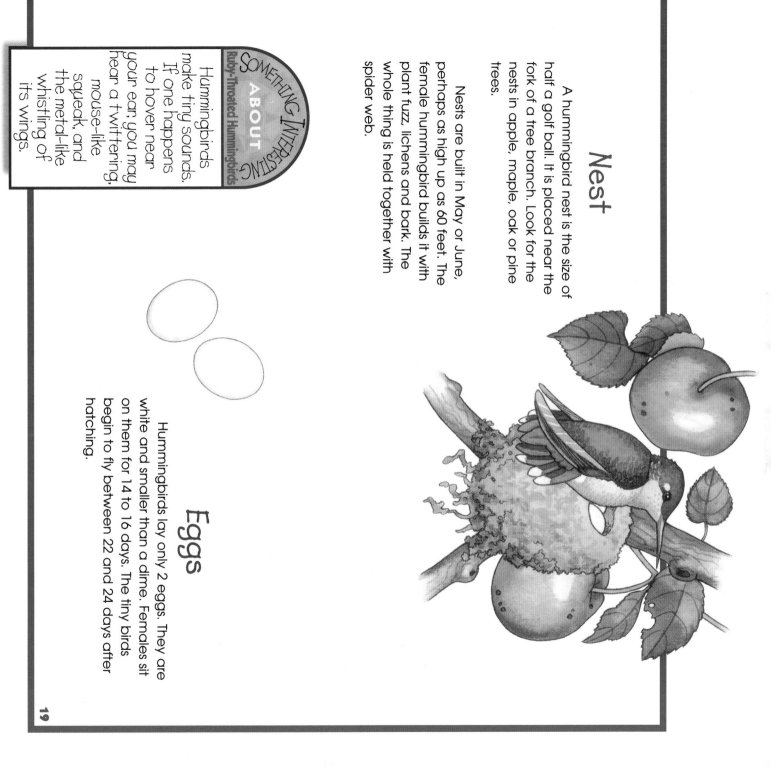

Eggs

Hummingbirds lay only 2 eggs. They are white and smaller than a dime. Females sit on them for 14 to 16 days. The tiny birds begin to fly between 22 and 24 days after hatching.

AMERICAN GOLDFINCH

Bird

Goldfinches seem to be happy birds, and their songs tell it. You will hear them in April and May, calling out "*potato-chips.*" But they don't eat potato chips, they really like thistle seeds. Goldfinches will stay around all summer if there are thistle seeds in a bird feeder—maybe even all winter.

Goldfinches swoop up and down as if on a roller coaster when they fly. They spend lots of time in flocks through June. They frolic about, singing, then eating, then singing and eating again, nonstop.

American goldfinches eat mostly seeds and a few insects. They are about as long as your hand and grow to be about 5 inches long.

The male is golden yellow, with a black cap tipped over his eyes, and black wings with white bars on them. In winter, he loses some of his bright coloring and looks the same as the female. She is mostly olive-yellow, with no black cap, less black on her wings and a whitish chest. By May, males turn gold again.

The nest is woven together so tightly that it would even hold water.

Nest

Goldfinches nest late in summer—July and August—in upright forks of bushes or small trees about 4 to 14 feet off the ground. They especially like to nest in apple, elm, maple, cottonwood, willow or pine trees, and roses or thistles.

The female builds the nest of fine grasses, bark and moss. Then it is lined with thistledown and silk from caterpillars.

Eggs

Goldfinches lay 4 to 6 blue-white eggs, smaller than pennies. The male brings the female food while she sits on the eggs. The eggs hatch in 12 to 14 days, and the babies can fly two weeks later. The young birds eat seeds already chewed by their parents.

RED-WINGED BLACKBIRD

Bird

The male red-winged blackbird looks like an army general. With red and yellow shoulder patches the black bird seems to screech out orders: "*Oaka-LEE!*" His calls are squeaky sing-songs.

The female looks dressed like a soldier, in dull browns and white on her wings and chest. She speaks with shorter, softer whistles, "*Tee-tee-tee-tee-tee.*" Red-winged blackbirds grow to be 7 to 9 inches long.

Redwings usually settle in marshy spots and they eat weed and marsh plant seeds, insects and fruit. They might even visit your feeder as early as March.

SOMETHING INTERESTING ABOUT Red-Winged Blackbirds

They gather in flocks to migrate south for winter. Blackbird flocks are famous. One bird watcher saw a flock of 30,000 black-birds flying.

Nest

Red-winged blackbirds build nests around cattail stalks from late April to early July. The female may use swamp milkweed strips wound around the stalks to make a cradle to hang her nest in. Into this she presses a deep cup of coarse grasses, lined with fine grass.

If you are near a redwing's nest, both male and female will cry out, "*Check!*" or "*Tseeeri!*" — their danger calls. Also, the female will fly straight up from the nest when startled.

Red-winged blackbird nests are also found in trees or thickets. These may be near the ground, or as high as 20 feet up in the tree.

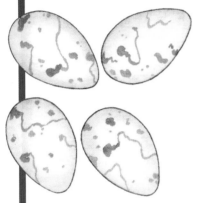

Eggs

The eggs are blue-green, with streaks, blotches and spots of purple, black or brown. The spots wash off if the eggs get wet. Only the female incubates the eggs. The 3 to 5 quarter-size eggs hatch in 11 days—and 11 days later the new redwings can fly.

BARN SWALLOW

Bird

Barn swallows make flying look easy. They can even eat while flying. They fly low over water and splash into it when they want a quick bath.

Both male and female barn swallows are red, white and blue. Their face is reddish, a white band circles the back of their neck and their heads and backs are blue. Their belly is rusty-colored. A third of their body length is tail, with a wide fork at the end. They are about 6 to 7 inches long.

Barn swallows make a musical twitter most of the time. It sounds like they are chattering to music: "*tswit-tswit, tswit-tswit.*" Listen and watch for them to come swooping and looping your way late in April or early May. In September they will dash and dart away.

Nest

Barn swallows make their nests almost entirely of mud. They stick them to ledges outside or inside buildings from May to July using more mud. It is plastered in small dabs with straw between layers. The nest is lined with grass and feathers, and is only as big as half a teacup. It may be just above your head, or up to 20 feet from the ground.

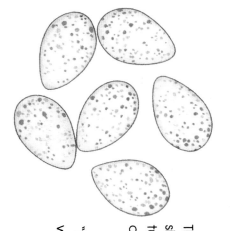

Eggs

Barn swallows lay 3 to 6 penny-size eggs. They are white with brown spots. Both parents sit on the eggs for about 2 weeks. They take turns bringing food to the babies until they can fly at 3 weeks old.

Barn swallows, like most birds, have a "hatching patch" on their tummy, a bare, warmer spot for the eggs.

GIVE THE BIRDS A SHOWER-BATH

Birds need water to drink—and to play in! Some birds love to run through a lawn sprinkler, or even a drippy water faucet. Here's a way to give them some water fun, and you a lot of bird watching fun.

WHAT YOU NEED

▶

- An old pail with a small leak, or punch a small hole in the bottom.

- An old pie pan or plastic pail lid that is shallow, no deeper than 1 or 2 inches. Or use an old garbage-can lid.

WHAT TO DO

▶

1 Hang the pail from a tree limb that is low enough for you to reach.

2 Underneath it, place the pan or lid.

3 Fill the hanging pail with water so that it drips water in the pool underneath.

Now stand back and bird watch. You may
be surprised to see how many different
kinds of birds will come running—and
flying—for a shower-bath. After all, birds
like to keep cool on a hot day too!

SPECIAL TIPS

If you don't have an old bucket,
try hanging a garden hose on
the tree limb over the pan.

Turn the water on so it just
trickles, and makes a little splash.

BLACK-CAPPED CHICKADEE

Bird

A chickadee is sitting on a branch when a bug flies by. The bird drops off backward, catches the bug in mid-air, does a somersault, and lands on its feet. Chickadees are bird-world acrobats!

The chickadee has a tiny beak made for digging into cracks for bug eggs no bigger than pinheads. They also like sunflower seeds, suet and finely cracked corn.

A black-capped chickadee weighs no more than four pennies. They have black caps and black bibs, with white faces and chests. Males and females look the same, and are about 5 inches long. You can hear them calling "*CHICKA-dee-dee-dee!*" all year long.

Little chickadees stay warm in winter because they have downy feathers right next to their skin—like thermal underwear. Their outer feathers are like a winter overcoat. Chickadees flit around even on below-zero winter days.

Chickadees are such good bug-finders that other birds, like nuthatches and woodpeckers, follow them to find bugs.

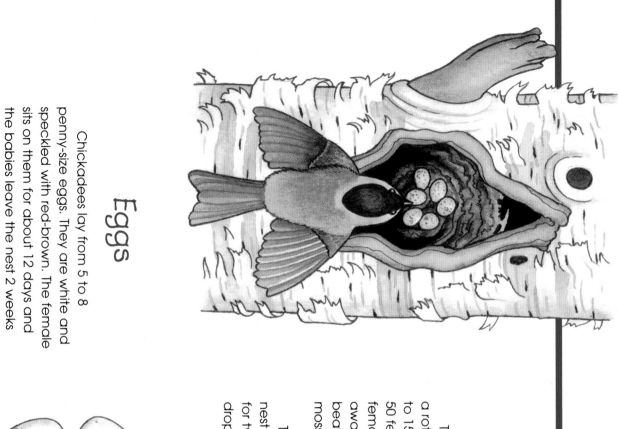

Nest

The chickadee's nest is usually in a rotted tree branch or stump, from 4 to 15 feet up—sometimes as high as 50 feet. April to June, the male and female dig out a nest by carrying away the rotted wood, beakful by beakful. They line the hollow with moss, plant down, hair, fur and wool.

The best way to find a chickadee nest (April through June) is to watch for two chickadees that perch and drop wood chips from their bills.

Eggs

Chickadees lay from 5 to 8 penny-size eggs. They are white and speckled with red-brown. The female sits on them for about 12 days and the babies leave the nest 2 weeks later.

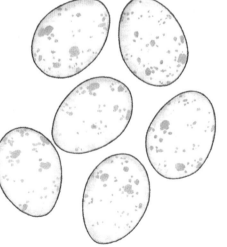

DOWNY WOODPECKER

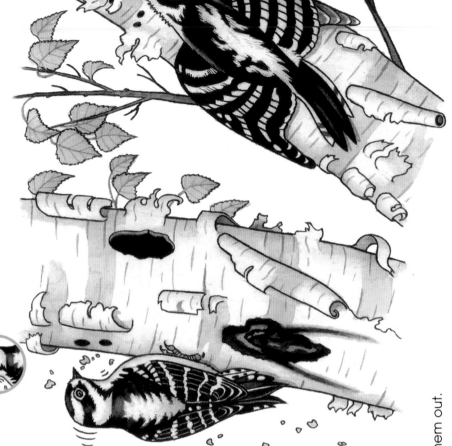

Bird

The downy woodpecker has been called "a friendly jackhammer." It is the smallest and tamest of the woodpeckers. If you walk up to a tree trunk it is on, it usually won't fly away. It scoots up behind the tree, and maybe it will peek around the tree at you. Downies make a light "keek keek" sound, and another sound like the whinny of a tiny horse.

The downy woodpecker's beak is like a chisel, flat and sharp, not pointed like most bird beaks. Downies find food by tapping the tree. The woodpecker hears bugs moving inside the tree and chisels them out.

The downy is black and white, with a white stripe down its back, and white stripes on its wings. Males have a patch of red on the back of their heads.

Downy woodpeckers nest in the holes of trees old enough to have large dead limbs, in April or May. To find one, listen for continual hammering, rather than short tapping that other birds make. Also look for wood chips at the base of the tree.

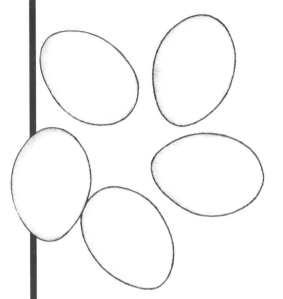

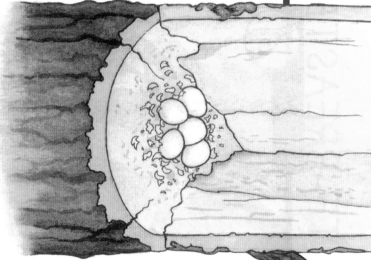

Nest

The entrance to the downy's hole is as big as a half-dollar, and opens into a hollow inside. The hollow is about as big as a football. There is no nest, except a few wood chips. Downy nests are built between 5 and 40 feet above the ground.

Eggs

Downy woodpecker eggs are about penny-size. Usually there are 4 or 5, and they are pure white. Both parents incubate the eggs equally, for about 12 days. In about 3 weeks, the new woodpeckers start to fly.

WHITE-BREASTED NUTHATCH

Bird

The nuthatch could be called an upside-down bird. It zigzags down a tree trunk head-first. It stops, points its head straight out from the tree, and calls *"Yank, yank!"* It sounds like a little toy horn.

The little white-breasted nuthatch is blue-gray, with a turned up bill. The male's cap is jet-black; the female's is lighter and more silvery. That is the only color difference between them. Nuthatches are 5 to 6 inches long.

As it hops down the bark, it nips and nabs beetles, ants and other insects and their eggs, as well as caterpillars, spiders and flies. It also eats acorns, hickory nuts and beechnuts.

The nuthatch stashes parts of the bugs it finds under bark. They are saved for later—maybe winter—in its "bark bank."

Nest

Nuthatches make nests in knot holes with wood rotted out behind them, in April to June. The male carries bark, twigs, grass, feathers and hair to the door. The female makes the nest. She stacks up bark, then weaves the other materials into a "mattress."

You will usually find the white-breasted nuthatch's nest in a big shade tree, from 5 to 50 feet off the ground.

Eggs

Nuthatch eggs are white and speckled with brown. They are a little bigger than pennies. There are 4 to 10 eggs per nest. The female sits on the eggs constantly, seldom flying out, even to eat. They hatch in 12 days. In 2 weeks, the newborns learn to climb down the tree like their parents, head-first. Then they learn to fly.

MAKE A HANG-DOWN SUET FEEDER

Many birds seldom feed at regular feeders.

But they love beef suet, and using a net bag—the kind that fruit and vegetables sometimes come in—you can give them a treat.

WHAT YOU NEED

▶

- Suet. It is a solid white beef fat. If you ask at a meat counter and tell them you want it to feed the birds, they might even give it to you for free. It comes in smaller or bigger chunks—either is okay.

- A net bag. It is the kind that onions, potatoes, and sometimes apples and oranges come in.

- About 2 feet of string.

WHAT TO DO

▶

1 Put 3 small pieces and 3 big pieces of suet in the net bag.

2 Bunch the bag's top together and tie one end of the string tightly around it.

3 Tie the other end of the string around a tree branch or railing that is strong enough to hold the bag.

SPECIAL TIP

▶

If your bag already has pull-handles, pull them tight and tie one end of the string through the loops.

OTHER THINGS TO DO

▲

Roll the suet in different kinds of birdseed. See which kinds the birds like best.

You can use different colored bags.

Make notes in the back of this book about which birds come to the feeder, and what seeds and color of bags they like best – or don't like.

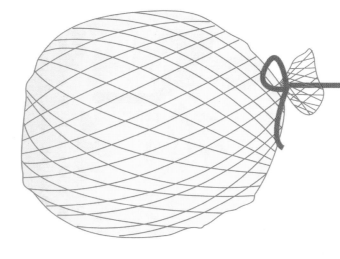

The suet feeder works best in winter, when the birds can't find much food outdoors. If you hang the suet bag up in the summer, be sure to refill it with fresh suet about once a week, so it doesn't spoil before the birds eat it all up.

MEADOWLARK

Bird

When a meadowlark crouches quietly in weeds that match its back feathers, it seems to vanish. When it stands up and puffs out its chest, it looks like a yellow flag. Its upper parts are brown-streaked and it has a brilliant yellow chest with a black V on it. Male and female meadowlarks look alike, but the female's colors are a little duller. Meadowlarks are between 8 and 11 inches long.

The Eastern meadowlark sings a high, slurry "See-you, see-yeeeer." The Western meadowlark sings out a lower, louder, longer, more flute-like song.

Meadowlarks have beaks that are long and strong. Meadowlarks use their beaks to poke into bug holes for dinner. They live in grassland and only eat seeds in the harsh winter.

You will hear the meadowlark when it arrives in late March or early April, singing from fence posts.

Nest

A meadowlark nest is hard to find. But these birds are fun and easy to watch if you do find a nest, because it is on the ground. The female builds it of grasses and weeds. She hides it by building a grass dome over the top and never flies down to it. She tunnels under the weeds to get to it. If you get too close, she will call out a warning "*Dzert!*"

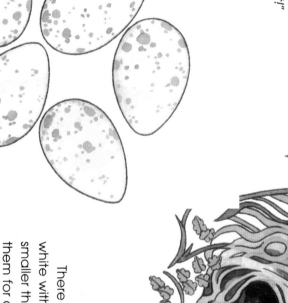

Eggs

There are usually 5 meadowlark eggs, white with brown or purple spots—a little smaller than a half-dollar. The female sits on them for about two weeks. In 11 to 12 days, the meadowlark babies can fly.

MOURNING DOVE

They put very little lining in the nest. It is so thin that eggs can be seen through the twigs from below.

Bird

The mourning dove is a gentle, peaceful bird. It calls "*Ooah, cooo, cooo, coo.*" You can also hear the whistling of its wings as it flies.

Mourning doves eat seeds, especially corn and sunflower seeds. They have long, pointy tails and small round heads. They are gray on top and the color of a fawn beneath—their soft colors seem to glow. Mourning doves are about 12 inches long. Males and females look alike, though the female is a little smaller, and duller in color.

The best time to see mourning doves is April to July mornings when they are nesting. Look for doves carrying twigs in their beaks.

Nest

The mourning dove nest is a loose jumble of sticks laid on a branch in low bushes or a tall tree. Their nest is on the ground sometimes. Most often they build it between 3 and 30 feet off the ground. Both male and female build it, between late May and late July.

Though mourning doves prefer nesting in evergreens, look for them also in apple, elm, maple, oak and willow trees.

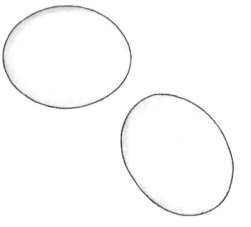

Eggs

Mourning doves usually lay 2 white eggs, each a little bigger than a quarter. The parents spend equal time incubating them for 2 weeks.

The young doves are fed "pigeon milk." It is a white, cheesy liquid made in the parents' stomachs from seeds they eat. It's pumped from their stomachs to their beaks and into the babies' bills. The babies can fly in 2 weeks.

KILLDEER

SOMETHING INTERESTING **ABOUT** Killdeers

It looks so much like the ground around it that you could be standing right over it, and not even see it.

Bird

This bird won't let you forget its name. It shouts it at you: "*Killdeer!*" The killdeer is one of the world's noisiest birds.

Besides its call, the best way to recognize a killdeer is by the black double necklace around its neck. It is dark brown on top and white on the bottom. It eats earthworms and insects. Males and females look alike, and are between 9 and 11 inches long.

The killdeer is famous for its "broken-wing" trick. If you come near its nest, it hobbles away with wings dragging, crying as if its wing is broken. A killdeer does this to draw you away from the nest. When you leave, the clever bird returns to its nest.

Killdeers migrate in October, and are some of the earliest birds to come back in March.

Nest

Killdeers are very sneaky nesters. Their nest is hardly even a nest. It is just a shallow hollow on the ground with stones and a little grass around it.

To find the killdeer's nest, put a marker where you first saw the bird and walk in a spiral around the marker, each circle a little farther from it. Watch carefully up to 100 feet from the marker—you should eventually find it.

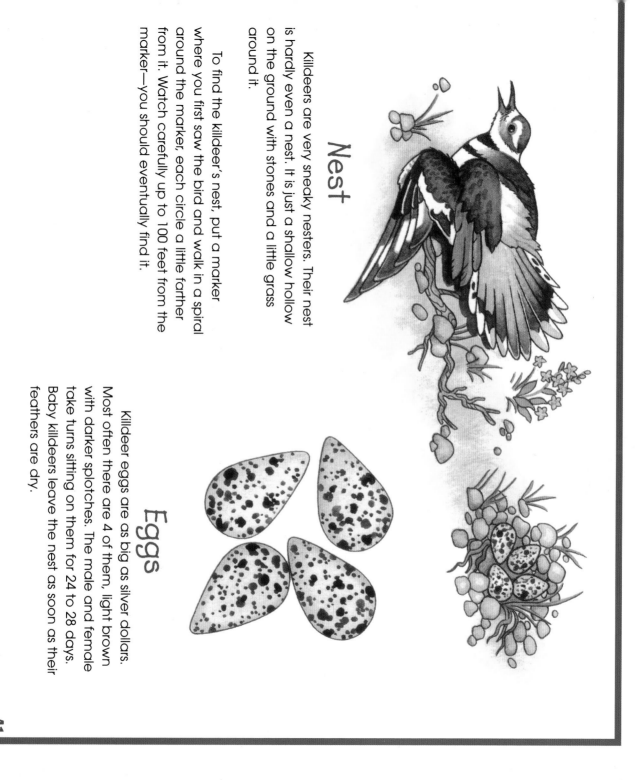

Eggs

Killdeer eggs are as big as silver dollars. Most often there are 4 of them, light brown with darker splotches. The male and female take turns sitting on them for 24 to 28 days. Baby killdeers leave the nest as soon as their feathers are dry.

SCRAPBOOK

Birds, Nests and Eggs

Find All Kinds of Stuff . . .

Take-Along Guides

Titles available in the Take-Along Guide series:

Berries, Nuts and Seeds
ISBN 978-1-55971-573-7

Birds, Nests and Eggs
ISBN 978-1-55971-624-6

Caterpillars, Bugs
and Butterflies
ISBN 978-1-55971-674-1

Flamingos, Loons
and Pelicans
ISBN 978-1-55971-943-8

Frogs, Toads and Turtles
ISBN 978-1-55971-593-5

Planets, Moons and Stars
ISBN 978-1-55971-842-4

Rabbits, Squirrels
and Chipmunks
ISBN 978-1-55971-579-9

Rocks, Fossils
and Arrowheads
ISBN 978-1-55971-786-1

Seashells, Crabs
and Sea Stars
ISBN 978-1-55971-675-8

Snakes, Salamanders
and Lizards
ISBN 978-1-55971-627-7

Tracks, Scats and Sign
ISBN 978-1-55971-599-7

Trees, Leaves and Bark
ISBN 978-1-55971-628-4

Wildflowers, Blooms
and Blossoms
ISBN 978-1-55971-642-0

NORTHWORD
Minnetonka, Minnesota